Caldbeck

Jenny Pagdin
Caldbeck

 **Lorgnette** Series

First published in 2017
by Eyewear Publishing Ltd
Suite 333, 19-21 Crawford Street
Marylebone, London W1H 1PJ
United Kingdom

Typeset with graphic design by Edwin Smet
Printed in England by Lightning Source
All rights reserved © 2017 Jenny Pagdin

The right of Jenny Pagdin to be identified as author of this work has been asserted in accordance with section 77 of the Copyright, Designs and Patents Act 1988

ISBN 978-1-912477-33-3

Eyewear wishes to thank Jonathan Wonham for his generous patronage of our press.

WWW.EYEWEARPUBLISHING.COM

For my son and for Leah

TABLE OF CONTENTS

9   DEFINITION OF LOVE
10 ON WHOM THE RAIN COMES DOWN
11 HINDSIGHT
12 NIGHT CROSSING (I) *Labour*
13 BEFORE THE POSTNATAL PSYCHOSIS
14 'BOY OF JENNY PAGDIN'
15 PRODROME
16 CRISTA
17 WHAT TO PACK FOR THE CALDBECK MOTHER & BABY UNIT
18 THE RADIO TIMES
19 INSANITY
19 SANITY
20 BANGED UP
21 NIGHT CROSSING (II) *Insomnia*
22 METAMORPHOSIS
23 THERAPY IS LIKE SORTING THE LINEN CUPBOARD
24 RELAPSE
25 COTTAGE GARDEN
26 CRACKPOTS
27 NAÏVE FAMILY PORTRAIT
28 DEFINITION OF HOPE

30 ACKNOWLEDGEMENTS

DEFINITION OF LOVE

Old English, related to leave and lief

Verbal noun: something known by its actions
(as the wind is), noun: nothing (in a contest);
the press of breath against a diver's chest
(symptoms include insomnia, digestive tension);
the invisible movement of lips on
lips forgetting to breathe. Verb trans: to be possessed
beyond all reason: not by one as he really exists
but he as if remade by your devotion.
Verb intrans: to be one with the birds in flight
and one with the deer that skits across the forest floor;
to touch skin along warm skin and make no break
unless he turns in sleep (cf. bulbs at night
that gleam in the darkened greenhouse, warm and sure;
nubbed roots which intertwine in earth). Antonym: heartache.

ON WHOM THE RAIN COMES DOWN
Title from Thomas Hardy's 'An Autumn Rain-Scene'.

People do say never to touch a tent
that's heavy with water;
I barely even knew a woman could
get ill and hurt her child.

They said our baby could have Downs,
for six months our odds were pencilled on the wardrobe,
while my auntie, cousins, friends,
succumbed to cancers, fraud or death.

They said our baby might have infantile hypotonia,
then he fainted and wouldn't come round,
I was sick and fainted and was sick, sick, sick
and still it rained down, crosshatching the sky.

HINDSIGHT

As we walked through the cemetery
we talked about her painting – a test,
I realised later. She was unimpressed
with my defence of her day job, keeping her huge shades on
though dusk was falling. I had my fingers on
the rose quartz she'd given me (just for fun, she stressed)
– a talisman. She didn't seem distressed
and my mind was more on you.

Then morning sickness in the car and plane,
the heat of the walls, the terracotta floor.
They told me it happened just after we went.
Pictures spilling from her car. That train.
And continuing with you, my child, I wasn't sure
how to protect you from my torment.

NIGHT CROSSING (I)
Labour

And when she took away the gas & air I didn't
know how I'd get across to the next one,
heavy, pressed bare against the rails, my hand
still grasping for the mask. I never cried
until she stitched me up – *it's like a jigsaw*
you beached upon my chest – they called it *latching*,
they called it *colostrum*, my tea and toast gone cold.

BEFORE THE POSTNATAL PSYCHOSIS

A mother holds the closed hand
of her sleeping newborn –
his small body enough

'BOY OF JENNY PAGDIN'

Navel clamped like a sandwich bag
forehead wax-red
wild arms stir the air. Branches.

PRODROME
n. an early symptom indicating the first stages of an illness

The milk coming in:
two waterwheels churn
in my sleepless chest.

After week one: a café man
cracks a joke about baby brain.
I can't understand.

After week four, I am nauseous
from being still awake. And it still takes
till nine for dinner to be microwaved.

At six weeks: see my glee
while dreaming I can soothe the baby
by filling his cot with warm water.

The clock strikes twelve. This week: back to hospital
– not Maternity this time
but a reverse: the psychiatric ward.

CRISTA

Like the twin I never had, you came
calling unannounced, wheeling your bike
the differences between us slight –
China for Lebanon; making art, not poetry.
After the first year a train undid you;
my husband forbidden to see
the mosaic.
The second year I crossed an unmarked, unfenced railway track
in front of the unannounced 10:17
and later that morning forgot the existence of my baby –
trailing, like a refugee, my slummy-mummy scarves
– a rainbow in a doctors' bag –
to the psychiatric hospital
where the windows look out on indoors,
the doors (all locked) on bars and fences.

After the stigmata, it took the first week to have breakfast
the second to find my programme
the third week was packing, packing
and in the fourth, I wrote.
Finally broken – as a horse is broken in –
– undignified.

My indigo shawl, fractured wings.

From the herb patch
the cloud-fleeced sun
made a moon in one-way glass.

WHAT TO PACK FOR THE CALDBECK MOTHER & BABY UNIT

- at least one floaty evening dress
- Bach remedies in a floral case
- an empty purse for emergencies
- cheese, for parties
- a magic book that reads itself
- your true colours, and a heart to wear pinned to the outside of your sleeve
- a pair of slippers
- a list of false names, for your child.

THE RADIO TIMES

The TV in the hospital
is on all day. Cannot be switched off.
Too loud. Colours too saturated.

But every actor is someone you know
from the world outside, and the History Channel
is telling you what your Nan is like,

this week's Blind Date features your workmates,
wedding rings are 50p, with the key
to creation flashing up at you just before you watch the weather.

INSANITY

My mind blew open so wide, I couldn't trust the sun to set

SANITY

Was like trying to make a sandwich out of breadcrumbs

BANGED UP

Watching the sun set, eye to the key-
hole, night after night.
When I first arrived I still thought
I could astral travel,
or I thought I might follow clues to find treasure,
a merry hunt,
I never forced the ground-floor doors
(though I watched others fail at it
and I did call the fire brigade once).
I was starting to wonder if I would fly. It was finally
my mother who told me: look, *take responsibility
for the child*. And after that, I breezed it.

NIGHT CROSSING (II)
Insomnia

Making the terrible crossing till six a.m.
I chart a course through *Songs of Leonard Cohen*,
watching the window in the door,
turning my iPod wheel like a little helm,
and lie down with *The Sisters*, and *Suzanne*,
and find the lines for grief, the lines for shame,
and taste the small rain falling from my cheek
and breathe the thin stars rising through my lungs.

METAMORPHOSIS

Nervous breakdown sounds a little soft
for my liking, just as *cocoon*
and *chrysalis* are too aerial,
speaking nothing of the hard-shelled body bag
inside which a being privately disintegrates,
privately rebuilds.

I can never again be as I was
but the blood fills and strengthens my imago wings.

THERAPY IS LIKE SORTING THE LINEN CUPBOARD

You start with a crumpled tangle,
musty, unseemly and over-spilling,
always in sight, as the cupboard won't close.

You've got to scoop them all up, press them smooth,
spritz with lavender, lay them down,
finally shut that door, until you need something.

RELAPSE

To go mad again
is perhaps inevitable,
but I do not know when,

I do not want to run
the risk, however small,
of going mad again.

One in a hundred women and men:
I will suffer as do you all,
I do not know when

or if I should give up medication
(but when I consider it, I am appalled
to think I might go mad again).

Fish oil, therapy, documentation,
when it comes, I will happily try them all –
I do not know when.

I say my prayers loudly: Amen, Amen,
but I expect, despite it all,
to go mad again
though I do not know when.

COTTAGE GARDEN

When I imagine
Dr Bach at Mount Vernon,
his cup and saucer still lukewarm,
he is barefoot or leather-sandalled
among the dew and hollyhocks,
stooping to touch each simple,
and I want to believe, too, that God has touched
the antidote for each distress
into the flowers.

When I was at my worst,
gulping Rescue Remedy
couldn't help me. Nothing could.
But now, clematis brings me down to earth.
Clematis, which he recommends
for those *'not fully awake'*.
I think I believe in this.
(Old English *belyfan*. Literally, *to love*.)
Because I feel heard.

CRACKPOTS

Kintsugi: broken
pots mended with seams of gold
more valuable cracked

NAÏVE FAMILY PORTRAIT

Early months, changing
you, you peed on your own face
then laughed; you've started
drawing people now, the lines
and circles speaking to me,

stick figures with legs
on our chins, horizontal
hair above our heads.
We stand admiring our selves.
Perfect? Functional?

DEFINITION OF HOPE

Verb with infinitive: intend, if possible:
'she hoped to be heard'; 'he hoped to raise the child'.
Verb intrans: to want something to happen:
'they hoped for a long remission, perhaps till death'.
Count noun: 'his last hopes the tiny magic
of pills or seeds'. *Mass noun:* 'the hope we feel
as the butterfly crawls out, its wings still budded and moist';
Archaic: absolute trust. *Antonym:* nothing.

ACKNOWLEDGEMENTS

I am very grateful to the editors of Iota Magazine 87, Spring 2010, who published 'Definition of Love' under the title 'OE, related to leave and lief'.

Thanks to Julia Webb for the insightful support with these poems, and to my editor at Eyewear Publishing, Rosanna Hildyard, who has done such a wonderful job of improving the body of work.

I am also incredibly grateful to my poetry teachers: Avril Bruten, Todd Swift, George Szirtes, Lavinia Greenlaw and Denise Riley and to the many friends who have read and encouraged me over the years. Thanks to my husband for his patience and careful listening, and to my boy for the inspiration.